# DESERT BONEYARD

# DESERT BONEYARD

## DAVIS MONTHAN A.F.B. ARIZONA

### Philip Chinnery

**Motorbooks International**
Publishers & Wholesalers Inc
Osceola, Wisconsin 54020, USA ®

HIRTLE, 87

# Acknowledgements

Many people have helped and contributed to this book and I am indebted to the following:
Chris Allen
Henry F. Carter
Robert M. Cornwell, DDS
Duncan Cubitt and Ken Ellis of Key Publishing
Lt. Col. Robert A. Drewitt, USAF
Mary Gentry, Pima Air Museum
Lt. Col. William H. Greenhalgh, USAF (Ret)
Col. J. M. McCampbell, USAF (Ret)
Douglas D. Olson
Lindsay Peacock
Col. I. R. Perkin, USAF (Ret)
Alma P. Rice
Col. R. Frank Schirmer, USAF (Ret)
Col. C. L. Stafford, USAF (Ret)
836th Air Division Public Affairs Office
HQ USAF/PAO Magazines and Books Division.

This edition first published in 1987 by Motorbooks International, Publishers & Wholesalers, Inc, PO Box 2, 729 Prospect Avenue, Osceola, WI 54020, USA.

Desert Boneyard © Philip Chinnery
Published by Airlife Publishing Ltd., Shrewsbury, England in 1987

Printed and bound in the United Kingdom by Livesey Ltd., Shrewsbury.

United States Library of Congress Cataloging-in-Publication Data
Chinnery, Philip
    The desert boneyard.
    1. Aerospace Maintenance and Regeneration Center
    I. Title
    623.74'6'0288      UG634.5

ISBN 0-87938-263-5

# 1

# The early years and years of expansion

Following the collapse of Nazi Germany in May 1945 and the surrender of Japan after the atomic bomb attacks on Nagasaki and Hiroshima three months later, America's fleets of war-weary aircraft began to return home. By June 1946 almost 34,000 aircraft had arrived at thirty airfields throughout the United States. The majority of these, some 26,700 aircraft, were in storage at seven main airfields.

Clinton Naval Air Station in Oklahoma was packed with 8,028 Navy aircraft of 22 different types, including 1,444 Grumman Wildcats and 1,366 Hellcats. 5,660 aircraft were at Walnut Ridge, Arkansas, including 87 B-32s, nearly the entire production run, flown direct to the storage field from the factory at Fort Worth. Kingman Army Air Field in Arizona received over 5,500 aircraft. Around one third were B-17s and a third B-24s, with the rest made up of several types, including the A-20, B-25, B-26, P-38 and P-63. Ontario in California had 1,879 aircraft, parked neatly in rows including A-20s, B-26s and C-46 Commandos. Altus in Oklahoma had 2,543 aircraft in storage; Alberquerque, New Mexico, was host to 1,706 and Vernon in Texas 1,322. As the wartime training and transport units began in wind down, the numbers of aircraft in storage increased even more. The question now was what to do with them all?

The Chief of the Army Air Force, General 'Hap' Arnold, once said that the only way to get better aircraft after a war was to destroy the oldest models. He recalled the situation following the end of World War 1, when Congress insisted that the US Army Air Service continue to use the thousands of old aircraft left over from the war, rather than approve the funding of more modern types.

The development of the jet engine now rendered the bulk of the fighter types obsolete and a new bomber, the B-29 had taken over the role of the famous B-17 and B-24. There were also too many aircraft of all types, to fulfil the peace-time needs of the US armed forces. The aircraft manufacturers themselves, quite understandably, viewed the thousands of stored aircraft with horror. Their books were now full of cancelled orders and their production lines stilled. New types were on the drawing board and under development, and the future of their companies was far from certain.

Fortunately for the manufacturers and their workforces, the decision was made to scrap or sell to the private sector the bulk of the aircraft in storage. The War Assets Administration and the Reconstruction Finance Corporation were tasked with the disposal of over $9,900,000,000 worth of aircraft and soon $8,000,000 worth of aircraft was being scrapped every day.

By melting down the aircraft, approximately 65 to 70 per cent of the planes' metal could be recovered in ingot form. The most important metal in it was aluminium — 13,000 lb in a B-24 bomber. However, it could not be recovered as pure aluminium, but as an alloy and its possible industrial re-use and scrap-metal value was quite low.

Martin Wunderlich, a Jefferson City, Missouri, contractor, paid $2,780,000 for 5,437 of the aircraft stored at Kingman Field. By draining the remaining fuel from the aircraft he recovered his initial purchase price and soon three furnaces were operating, melting the aircraft themselves into ingots. One by one, the old warhorses met their fate: *Embarrassed,* a battle-scarred B-24 from the 'Flying Circus' of the 380th Bombardment Group, was one. It flew 108 missions with the Fifth Air Force in the Pacific, sank three Japanese ships and downed three enemy planes. *Hi-Ho Silver* was another; this B-17 took part in 130 bombing missions and bagged four Nazi planes.

Not many aircraft escaped the furnaces. The City of Athens, Georgia, purchased eleven aircraft for a memorial to its World War 2 flyers, and a handful of others, such as the B-29 *Enola Gay*, which dropped America's first atom bomb, were earmarked for preservation.

Although combat aircraft were theoretically unsaleable, B-25s were offered at $8,250, P-47s at $3,500 and B-17s at $13,750. Three of the latter mysteriously found their way to Israel and joined that country's fledgling air force.

By June 1947 the War Assets Administration had virtually completed its job of disposing of some 65,000 aircraft. 30,000 had been sold as scrap, for a return to the government of a cent and a half per pound, empty weight. The return on the sale of the 35,000 aircraft which could have been certificated for civilian flight use, was higher, at around eight per cent of their initial cost. These included 11,915 primary, 8,670 basic and 4,775 advanced trainers; 2,900 light, 1,300 medium and 450 heavy transports and nearly 4,000 liaison types. The last to be sold were 625 C-46 transport aircraft, which were offered for sale at between $10-15,000 each. The overall effect was to increase the number of civilian registered aircraft in America by one third, to 92,247 planes.

Despite the haste in which the bulk of America's war-fleet was disposed of, it was decided that a few types ought to be saved. The Iron Curtain was descending across Europe and the Cold War had begun. It would be prudent to keep some aircraft in reserve, just in case.

Warner Robin's Air Depot in Georgia; Victorville Army Air Field in California and Pyote Army Air Field in Texas were amongst the handful of bases chosen to store the aircraft required for preservation. Their existence was short-lived though, unlike that of Davis-Monthan Army Air Field in Arizona, which was also chosen as a storage area and is still in use today.

Davis-Monthan Field, located south-east of the City of Tucson, was formerly the city's municipal airport and was named after two Air Service officers from Tucson who were killed in separate aviation accidents in the early 1920s; Lieutenants Samuel H. Davis and Oscar Monthan. The main reasons for its choice as a storage centre were the low annual rainfall of eleven inches per year, the low humidity of between ten and twenty per cent and the type of soil present in that part of the Sonora Desert. Known as 'caliche', the soil has a low acidic content, which is ideal for long-term storage of aircraft. The soil is also baked so hard that aircraft can be safely parked on it, without needing tarmac or concrete stands.

On 15 November 1945 Davis-Monthan Field was transferred from the 2nd Air Force of Continental Air Command to the jurisdiction of the San Antonio Air Technical Service Command (SAATSC) at Kelly Field, Texas. The 4105th Army Air Force Base Unit (Air Base) was activated at Davis-Monthan Field under the command of Colonel Herbert M. West, Jr, and by 10 January 1946 the first of 300 C-47s had arrived for long-term preservation and storage. 1,500 of the comparatively new Boeing B-29 Superfortress bombers were also earmarked for preservation, with around 700 destined for Davis-Monthan Field and the others to the storage centres at Warner-Robins, Victorville and Pyote Fields.

Lieutenant-Colonel R. F. Schirmer took over as commander of the 4105th on 13 September 1946. The Schirmer family quarters had been the base nursery building during World War 2 and their two young daughters were surprised to find the walls covered with caricatures of Mickey Mouse, Donald Duck and other Disney characters. Colonel Schirmer also had a surprise waiting for him; he found himself custodian of 713 B-29s, 363 C-47s and eighteen museum aircraft.

The name of the storage centre was amended one month later to the 4105th AAFBU (Aircraft Storage), which was more in keeping with its mission of receiving and processing aircraft for storage. Air Technical Service Command was renamed Air Material Command five months later, in March 1947.

The storage procedure was rather basic in those early days. On arrival the aircraft serial number would be noted, together with its general condition; the equipment on board would be listed and then the aircraft would be towed out to the storage location. It would then be put up on wooden blocks to take the weight off the tyres and inspected monthly for corrosion or damage.

There was so much space in the 2,000-acre storage area that the desert animals were not bothered too much by the inspection personnel. Sometimes, however, conflicts between animals and people did occur. One day, some of the inspectors cornered a bobcat inside the wheel-well of a parked B-29. Their first attempt at removing the cat from the wheel-well, by spraying it with a $CO_2$ fire extinguisher, was a failure. It just made the cat look like a snow owl. They tried fizzing a Coke bottle and squirting that into its eyes, but that only produced a lot of head shaking. Finally, someone produced a carbon tetrachloride extinguisher, and after a few shots of this chemical, the cat fell out of the wheel-well to be despatched by a blow to the head with a Coke bottle. One of the inspectors, who hunted a lot, took out a large knife and skinned the bobcat in a flash.

Opposite: Boeing B-29 Superfortress 'Bockscar' dropped the second Atomic bomb on Nagasaki on 9 August 1945. It was stored with other museum aircraft at the 4105th AAFBU after the war's end and is now preserved at the Air Force Museum. *(The Boeing Company)*

Above: Piled high due to lack of space, Air Force and Ohio Air National Guard F-84E Thunderstreaks await disposal in November 1958. *(Douglas D. Olson)*

Opposite: A fence of giant propellers borders the Convair B-36 Peacemaker fleet. With their engines removed they await their fate. *(USAF Photograph)*

On another occasion one of the field maintenance men sat down on the corner of one of the wooden platforms, supporting the landing gear of a B-29. He was reaching into his back pocket for his pencil when a bull snake struck at and bit his hand. Fortunately the snake was of a non-poisonous variety and the victim calmly stood up, stamped on the snake with his big cowboy boots and killed it. He then ambled several hundred yards to the first aid station and was taken to hospital for treatment.

By the end of 1946 the eighteen museum aircraft had been joined by a dozen others. The two B-29s which had the dubious distinction of dropping the atomic bombs on Japan were there; the *Enola Gay* and *Bocks Car*. The TB-24D Liberator *Strawberry Bitch* was also in storage, still wearing its desert camouflage. It had been the first B-24 to land in North Africa in late 1942. The Presidential plane used by Roosevelt and Truman, C-54A *Sacred Cow* had also been kept for the future Air Force Museum. Other types included a C-82N Packet; XC-38 Destroyer attack plane with 75 mm cannon in its nose; YP-61 Black Widow night fighter, together with a P-61B model; A-26C; B-32; A-20A, B-17G and a former Luftwaffe Junkers Ju-88. Seventeen more aircraft, namely a C-46A, C-87, B-24, XC-53A, C-45A, AT-7, B-25, RB-26C, XCG-17, XCG-15A, C-40A, C-60A, RB-17E, two C-47s and two TB-29s were dropped from the museum storage project in 1947-48 and scrapped a year later.

Apart from the museum aircraft which met their end in 1949, the one and only B-19 bomber was broken up at the same time. Until the advent of the B-36 it was the largest aircraft ever built for the Army Air Force and had been used as a flying test laboratory. It was 132 ft long, 41 ft high and had a wingspan of 212 ft. It would have made an impressive museum exhibit.

Each of the stored B-29s was worth over half a million dollars and to protect their investment the Army Air Force decided to cocoon them in airtight cases. The cocoons consisted of two layers of plastic and a sealer known as Insulmastic No 4500, a Gilsonite product. It was seven times stronger than rawhide and was designed to keep out dirt and moisture for at least ten years.

The Fort Pitt Packaging Company was awarded the contract to cocoon 486 of the 679 B-29s then in storage and work began in July 1947. Each aircraft was washed and then many bags of moisture-absorbing dessicant were placed inside them. The propellers and engine cowlings were covered with masking tape and a first coat of yellow plastic was applied by spray guns to the outside of the aircraft. This was followed by a second, red coat; the colour being changed to ensure correct coverage of all areas of the aircraft. The black insulmastic sealer followed and then a final coat of aluminium paint was applied to reflect most of the heat from the sun.

The Cocooning Project was terminated in May 1948 after 447 B-29s had been treated. Whilst the aircraft were now well protected from deterioration, the upkeep of the cocoons themselves, and their removal from aircraft required to fly again, were major headaches. At least fifty of the B-29s suffered from ballooning of the cocoons. This was caused by air trapped under the cocooning expanding during the heat of the day and breaking the seal of the plastic. This required the contractor to remove the blister and reapply all four coats of preservative. A greater problem surfaced in 1948 when attempts were made to remove the cocoons from eight B-29s required to return to service. If the air was too cold the brittle cocoons would break into small pieces and 600 man hours were required to strip the cocoons from each aircraft. These early attempts at aircraft preservation were lengthy and expensive and the Air Force, which became a separate entity under the Department of Defense in September 1947, was forced to seek alternative methods of protecting its stored aircraft.

The 4105th was renamed the 3040th Aircraft Storage Depot in August 1948 and reclamation and salvage was added to its mission. 47 B-29s were set aside for spare parts reclamation, together with the museum aircraft already mentioned. By the end of the year the number of aircraft in storage had dropped to 535 B-29s and 187 C-47s. One of the main reasons for this was the closure of all overland routes into Berlin in the summer of 1948. The Soviet attempt at brinkmanship led to the Berlin Airlift, by which the Allies supplied the city with a continuous stream of transport aircraft. Four Strategic Air Command Bomb Groups flew their B-29s to Germany and England, but fortunately they were not required to go to war.

Representatives from the Brazilian and Uruguayan Air Forces and the Colombian government, visited Davis-Monthan during 1949, to arrange for the procurement of C-47s under the Mutual Defence Assistance Program. At the same time the Air Force was experiencing a critical shortage of C-47 spare parts and by the end of the year the number of C-47s in storage had been halved to 84.

The year 1950 saw almost two-thirds of the B-29s return to service. 87 were to be loaned to the British Royal Air Force as a stop-gap measure between the demise of the ageing Lincolns and the arrival of the modern Canberra and V-bomber aircraft. They were designated Washington B Mk Is and the first four were handed over in March. Many came from USAF units and the others straight from storage, returning to the desert again in 1954.

The Korean War had begun in June and within two weeks Headquarters, Air Material Command, had ordered the withdrawal from storage of fifty B-29s for overhaul and reconditioning by the Grand Central Aircraft Company at Tucson Airport. As the 3040th's personnel rushed to comply with the request, the B-29s of the Far East Air Force Bomber Command were carrying out their first bombing raid, on the North Korean port of Wonsan.

By the end of 1950 SAC's B-29 force had increased by fifty per cent, to around 580 aircraft. To help supply the spare parts needed to maintain the force, the 3040th began to reclaim 27 more B-29s, recovering around $300,000 worth of parts from each $570,000 aircraft. However, this was just not enough and an accelerated reclamation programme was

In the immediate post-war years, large numbers of Douglas C-47 Skytrains were stored with the 4105th Army Air Force Base Unit, the forerunner of today's AMARC.
*(R. Frank Schirmer)*

initiated with the target of disassembling two B-29s per week by August 1951. This caused no end of problems, despite increasing the workforce from 231 to 359. The unit possessed only one electric crane and two forklift trucks; there was a shortage of Aerostands and problems with the handling of the heavy main landing gears. After removal, the landing gear was usually towed away by a wreck truck, but this hazardous practice had to stop and a dolly was constructed to which the gear could be strapped and towed safely.

The centre of gravity of a B-29 changed drastically after disassembly, so fifteen-feet-long, one foot-square timbers were tied to the nose wheel-well and as many as 25 personnel loaded into the nose section compartments to balance the aircraft, while it was towed one and a half miles back to the storage area for de-militarisation, prior to sale as scrap. This basically involved removing the tail section of the aircraft; heavy cables would be looped over the tail assembly by a crane and attached to a heavy cleat track. The track would take off fast and the cable would contract around the fuselage, slicing the 6,000 lb tail assembly off, dropping it on to a trailer underneath. Parts removed from the tail assemblies prior to their destruction included tail turret, horizontal and vertical stabilisers, bullet-proof glass, bottom turret, tail skid and oxygen tanks. It was later decided to cut off the tail sections before the removal of the weight forward of the centre of gravity, to balance the aircraft, and this was done with favourable results.

From B-29 *42-63472* over 1,750 parts were removed, with a total value of $354,606, including its bomb sights, engines, fuel and oil tanks, propellers and instruments. The four-bladed propellers were crated and shipped to Tinker Air Force Base (AFB), Oklahoma, for overhaul and each one thus reused saved the government $5,300. Even the B-29 carcasses were being sold for scrap at $2,300 each.

The Priority Reclamation Project was completed by February 1952 and there was now more time available to prepare aircraft for departure. Almost forty B-29s were flown out to depots for overhaul prior to returning to service, and at the end of the year only 136 cocooned and 47 non-cocooned B-29s were left in storage.

Strategic Air Command was now taking delivery of the modern B-47 Stratojet bomber, supplementing the B-36s and B-50s already in service. From now on, life for the B-29 was all downhill. On 1 April 1953 the HQ Air Material Command dropped a bombshell on the 3040th. Their recent efforts at reclaiming and returning B-29s to service notwithstanding, they were told to prepare for the arrival of 440 B-29s, as the type was now declared obsolete.

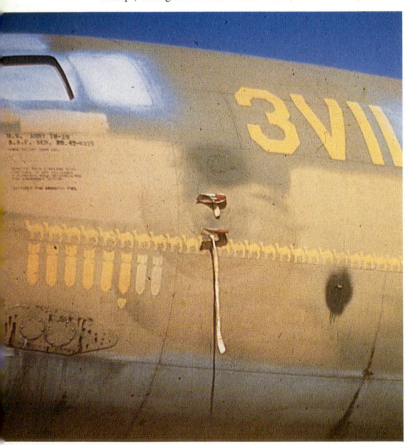

The mission requirements of the 3040th changed considerably during 1953. They were now to: (a) store and maintain aircraft in storage; (b) remove aircraft from storage and prepare for one-time flight; and (c) perform aircraft reclamation. These were in addition to various secondary missions, such as performing field maintenance work at other air bases.

In July, as the war in Korea drew to an uneasy close, the first 24 B-29s arrived out of the planned 440. By the end of the year 100 had arrived and the Air Force began to establish an Emergency War Reserve of B-29s at Davis-Monthan.

For the first time, aircraft other than B-29s and C-47s began to arrive, raising the number of aircraft in storage from 210 to 981 by the end of the year. These other types included 160 T-6 Texan trainers, which remained in service in USAF pilot schools until mid-1956; 29 SA-16A (later HU-16) Albatross amphibians which had been used by the Military Air Transport Service (MATS) Air Rescue Service since 1947 and were also used by the Navy and Coast Guard; 21 QB-17 Flying Fortress radio-controlled drones, used for air-to-air and ground-to-air target practice, and thirteen L-20 (later U-6) Beavers, single-engine monoplanes carrying a pilot and seven passengers.

The increasing numbers of aircraft arriving demanded a larger storage area and a further 480 acres were cleared and fenced, expanding the centre to 1,290 acres.

As the weeks passed aircraft arrived, departed or were reclaimed for spare parts. No sooner had a project been started, than it was changed again. It soon became obvious that the organisational abilities of those in command at HQ AMC and HQ USAF were somewhat lacking.

Early in 1954 HQ USAF directed that the FEAF Bomber Command be disbanded and its three B-29 wings were returned to the States and re-equipped with B-47s. 168 more B-29s had arrived for storage by June, although steps were now being taken to dispose of them as fast as they arrived.

Ten B-29s were dismantled and shipped to the New Mexico Institute of Mining and Technology at Scocorro, for Navy vulnerability tests. In 1982 visitors to the institute were amazed to find the remains of a B-29 amongst other hulks, still wearing RAF roundels. Presumably this was one of the 'Washingtons' that had been returned to the States after its RAF service and was one of the ten to be shipped there nearly thirty years before.

In August 1954 a 'blast test' commenced, involving ninety reclaimed B-29s. This was carried out by Army experts from the Aberdeen Proving Grounds in Maryland, using the 'latest developments in explosives'. After the explosions, the unit fire truck would extinguish any fires and studies would be made to assess the vulnerability and effectual damage to structural areas of the aircraft. The Army also took some B-29s back to the Aberdeen Proving Grounds because at least eight were found there in reasonable condition years afterwards, and at least four have since departed to museums.

Strategic Air Command's last B-29A, from the 307th Bomb Wing, arrived at Davis-Monthan on 4 November. In the same month a Navy representative from Inyokern, California, arrived to arrange the removal of a number of B-29s by one-time flight to the Navy Ordnance Proving Grounds at China Lake, California. The author photographed the last five survivors in 1984.

At the end of 1954, 463 B-29s were in storage and only eighty KB-29 tanker aircraft remained in service with SAC. Even these were slowly being replaced by the KC-97 Stratotanker. Over the next eighteen months the 3040th had its hands full with other types of aircraft arriving. 600 T-6s and 200 B-50 bombers were programmed to arrive and before long 75 of the B-50Ds would be flown out again, for conversion to KB-50 tankers by Hayes Industries in Birmingham, Alabama.

In June 1956 the 3040th was renamed the Arizona Aircraft Storage Branch. By this time 120 of the B-29s had been scrapped and 346 were still in storage. It took a further two years to scrap the rest of the B-29 fleet, but in the meantime the spotlight shifted from the B-29 to the massive B-36 Peacemaker.

The giant B-36 with its six pusher engines mounted behind the wings and a pair of jet pods under the wings, began to arrive at the AASB in the summer of 1956. Ten GRB-36Ds were amongst the first to arrive, followed by the RB-36Ds and Es of the 99th Strategic Reconnaissance Wing (SRW) and B-36Ds of the 92nd Bomb Wing. Almost immediately a reclamation project began, to strip usable parts from the first arrivals and return them to Air Force stocks for use on Peacemakers still in service. 39 B-36s were released to MarPak Corporation, under contract to the Air Force, for reclamation and removal of certain items, such as engines, rudders and flaps. Soon, stripped-out carcasses began to litter the desert and with more Peacemakers arriving each week, a smelter was brought into action to dispose of the unwanted hulks.

To try to plan the AASB's workload better, Air Material Command instructed them to perform a processing and reclamation service test on ten B-36s to determine how many man-hours were needed to reclaim each aircraft. At 10:45 on 3 June 1957, B-36F *49-2681* rolled to a halt at the end of the Davis-Monthan runway and was met by AASB personnel. It was then defuelled to 1,000 gallons and towed to the

industrial area where all loose inventory items were removed, along with the armament and specialised equipment. The rest of the fuel was drained, together with all oils and the aircraft was parked and tied down.

The 'save lists' were consulted and engineers went to work removing the parts required, including tyres and propellers. These were then cleaned, inspected and shipped out to various storage depots. Finally, the fire extinguisher systems were disarmed and the oxygen system pressure released. Within a matter of sixteen days *49-2681* had been transformed from a first-line strategic bomber to a derelict carcass.

The test proved that 942 man-hours were needed, on average, to reclaim a B-36, at a cost of $2,283. To reclaim all ten of the test aircraft cost $28,930 in labour and materials, but 7,106 items weighing a total of 500,000 lb were removed and saved, with a stock value and saving to the taxpayer of $7,750,000.

Other new types had begun to arrive, such as the ageing B-26 Invader and early-model jet fighters such as the F-80, F-84 and F-86, plus the eleven surviving C-74 Globemaster 1s of MATS. Another change had been the transfer of the surplus aircraft sales responsibility from the AASB Disposal Office to the Surplus Property Branch of the San Bernadino Air Material Area, who would send out invitations to bid on the carcasses no longer required. Foreign military sales came to the fore again in 1957 with B-26s departing for Brazil and 355 T-6 trainers going to foreign governments, including 180 T-6Gs sold to the French government.

The accelerated phase-out of aircraft from the active Air Force inventory over this period led to a huge increase in the number of aircraft arriving for storage. Over 900 B-29, B-36 and B-50 carcasses were on hand and there were so many F-84E and G fighters awaiting disposal that they were stacked three or four high. By 30 June 1958 a total of 3,943 aircraft, including carcasses, were on the AASB inventory. 3,141 aircraft had arrived over the preceding 12 months, as follows:

| | | | | |
|---|---|---|---|---|
| B-25 | . . . . . . . 605 | | F-80 | . . . . . . . 297 |
| B-26 | . . . . . . . 148 | | F-84 | . . . . . . . 370 |
| B-36 | . . . . . . . 101 | | F-86 | . . . . . . . 267 |
| B-47 | . . . . . . . 114 | | F-89 | . . . . . . . 100 |
| B-45 | . . . . . . . 4 | | F-94 | . . . . . . . 421 |
| B-50 | . . . . . . . 5 | | H-13 | . . . . . . . 29 |
| C-45 | . . . . . . . 124 | | H-21 | . . . . . . . 5 |
| C-46 | . . . . . . . 206 | | P-2 | . . . . . . . 14 |
| C-54 | . . . . . . . 31 | | T-28 | . . . . . . . 299 |
| C-124 | . . . . . . . 1 | | | |

Air Force Project 'Streamline 111R' involved the withdrawal from service of some 7,000 aircraft by the end of 1961. They had been declared excess to USAF operational requirements and the peak of the phase-out was to occur in 1959 and early 1960. In order to create the extra space needed for the aircraft due to arrive under 'Streamline 111R', the disposal operation at AASB moved into top gear. Soon three civilian smelters were in operation, under contract to the Air Force. One was operated by Aircraft Associates and was going full blast, trying to dispose of forty B-50s and 265 B-29s. The other two were owned by Page Airways and Marpak and concentrated on the 230 acres of B-36 carcasses. Alongside the contractors' smelters their guillotines were working overtime. These huge blades consisted of 8,500 lb of armour plate, dropped from a height of 75 ft from the boom of a crane, to sever parts of the aircrafts' wings and fuselage and cut them into easily handled pieces to feed into the smelters.

In May 1958 a sale was held to dispose of 65 B-36s and 550 other aircraft, but the smelter operators had their hands full and the aircraft remained unsold. All the time more aircraft were arriving and the latter half of the year saw 850 more processed into storage, including 185 B-25s and 255 C-45s. This brought the AASB inventory on 31 December 1958 to 4,326 aircraft, comprising 1,477 stored, 91 undergoing reclamation, 949 sold or awaiting sale and 1,809 carcasses. One sale which did go through was for thirty T-28s to the Mexican Air Force, and there was a lot of interest in the surplus T-6s and B-26s.

The year 1959 brought further changes to the mission requirements of the AASB. The responsibility for aircraft sales and disposal was transferred back to them from the SBAMA and an eighteen-man office was duly established. This not only handled sales of aircraft at Davis-Monthan but throughout the whole of the United States as well. The AASB was also given the task of redistributing excess USAF aircraft to other government agencies, Mutual Aid Program countries and other eligible transferees. Other surplus aircraft could now be donated to eligible groups or organisations, rather than facing automatic disposal in the hungry furnaces of the smelters.

Opposite: By the late 1950s the first jet fighters had arrived, including North American F-86L Sabres retired by the Air National Guard.
*(Douglas D. Olson)*

In the twelve months between June 1958 and June 1959, 1,652 more aircraft arrived at Davis-Monthan. These included 290 more B-25s, 411 C-45s, 232 F-86 Sabres, 211 T-28 trainers and 43· B-47 Stratojet bombers. One other interesting arrival was B-29 *45-21800* which had been modified to carry the experimental Bell X-1 aloft. It launched the X-1 around 200 times and on one occasion Captain Chuck Yeager became the first man to break the sound barrier in flight. The 432nd and last B-36 had also arrived and B-36 cot mattresses were on sale locally at $3.50 each. The last Peacemaker flight took place on 29 April 1959, when B-36J *52-2220* flew out of Davis-Monthan to the site of the new Air Force Museum at Wright-Patterson AFB.

On 1 August 1959 the Arizona Aircraft Storage Branch was redesignated the 2704th Air Force Aircraft Storage and Disposition Group and began to report directly to the HQ Air Material Command. In the same month 110 C-46 Commando cargo planes went on sale at Davis-Monthan, priced from $50,000 to $60,000 each. 94 B-26 twin-engine bombers were also put up for sale, at a fraction of the price, from $1,500 to $5,000 each.

More modern types of aircraft were beginning to arrive, such as the F-100, F-101, F-104 and F-105 from the Century series of fighters. The number of B-47 Stratojet bombers being retired was also increasing and the first B-57 Canberra and B-66 Destroyers had arrived. Hundreds of obsolete F-86 Sabres were coming in, together with early model KC-97 tankers. As the B-47s were being replaced by the B-52 Stratofortress, the KC-97s were also being replaced by Boeing's jet KC-135 Stratotanker. The change-over would take time though; SAC still possessed 27 Medium Bomb Wings equipped with B-47s and 33 Medium Air Refueling Squadrons with KC-97s.

By June 1960 4,072 aircraft were on the inventory of the 2704th. 1,777 had arrived during the preceding twelve months, including 120 B-47s, 163 C-45s, 463 F-86s, 202 F-89 Scorpions and 322 T-28s. However, the disposal rate had kept up with the arrivals and 1,000 aircraft had been broken up and scrapped over the same period. These included 375 F-84s, 215 F-94s, 207 F-86s and 42 B-36s. The last B-36 sale had taken place in May 1960 and included all remaining Peacemakers. This amounted to 2,800 tons of scrap metal and the lot was sold for $528,337 and sixty cents. It took a further seventeen months to process the carcasses through the smelters and the once mighty Peacemaker fleet ceased to exist.

The first of the mighty Convair B-36 Peacemakers arrived in 1956 and were all scrapped by 1962. Only five have survived the demise of the fleet. *(Douglas D. Olson)*

Many other aircraft were fortunate enough to leave the 2704th intact. 100 T-28s were supplied to the French government, together with ten B-26s. Peru received two B-57s, ten C-45Hs and two B-26s, while a further eight B-26s went to Guatemala. 49 aircraft were transferred to other Federal Agencies and 41 OH-13 Sioux helicopters were passed over to the Army. Two dozen aircraft, mostly C-45s, were also donated to various schools, towns and civil defence organisations for display or training purposes.

HQ Air Material Command had realised the potential value of its Davis-Monthan storage centre; $64 million worth of spare parts had been returned to the Air Force stocks between June 1959 and June 1960. Consequently a new industrial complex had been constructed and the work-force increased by over a hundred to 737 civilians and fourteen military by June 1961. 1,474 more aircraft had arrived including 301 B-47s, 474 F-86s and 296 T-33s. Despite this, the inventory had shrunk over twelve months from 4,067 to 2,922. This was mainly due to the amount of reclamation activity, which had reduced 1,845 aircraft to scrap. 257 aircraft were passed over to various government agencies and 508 more were sold to commercial concerns or foreign governments.

The Air Material Command had been split into two parts in April 1961, creating the Air Force Systems Command and the Air Force Logistics Command (AFLC). HQ AFLC was now the overseer of the 2704th and it was no doubt justifiably proud of its storage centre. Half a million dollars had been spent on a reclamation shelter, which not only kept the workers out of the desert sun, but provided 180,000 sq ft of shelter to house the reclamation processing, packaging and crating and shipping functions. Together with the new production line procedures, this contributed to the centre trebling the amount of spare parts returned to service, to $193,200,000. This was quite a substantial return on investment, considering that the budget for the 2704th was a mere $5,000,000 per year.

Opposite: Boeing KC-97F Stratotanker 51-0381 being scrapped following its replacement by the KC-135. C-97s have been stored, reclaimed and sold for scrap at Davis-Monthan AFB for more than 25 years. *(Author's Collection)*

Overleaf: The first Marine Corps Sikorsky CH-37C Mojave from Heavy Lift Squadron HMH-461 arrived for storage in December 1966. It was sold for scrap to Allied Aircraft Sales of Tucson in 1973. *(Robert M. Cornwell)*

In July 1961, with the US and Russia seemingly headed for a showdown on the Berlin question, President Kennedy delayed his previously directed accelerated B-47 phase-out programme, in order to improve the national defence posture. Six Bomb Wings and Six Air Refueling Squadrons had their deactivations postponed as a result. The 2704th was also coming to the end of 'Streamline 111R' and the number of arrivals between the summer of 1961 and 1962 dropped as a result to 691. A third of these, though, were C-47 Skytrain cargo aircraft, whose destiny lay not with the scrapper's torch but with a second career with commercial operators and foreign governments.

The Cold War intensified in October when a SAC U-2 spyplane brought back photographs of Soviet intermediate range ballistic missiles being installed on Cuba. On the 22nd, President Kennedy ordered an arms quarantine against further shipments destined for Cuba and demanded the removal of the missiles already there. He emphasised his demands by placing SAC's missiles and aircraft on full alert, armed with nuclear weapons.

The consequences at the 2704th were that all B-47 reclamation was stopped and plans were made to return a large number to service if required. Fortunately Russia agreed on the 28th to remove its missiles from Cuba, although it was too late for a U-2 pilot who was shot down by an anti-aircraft missile over Cuba the day before.

By the end of 1962 SAC had received the last of its B-52 and B-58 bombers and the retirement of the remaining B-47s could begin in earnest. The centre had now expanded to 1,744 acres, although many of these were vacant, and despite 804 more arrivals the inventory on 30 June 1963 stood at a 'mere' 2,734.

In 1964 the Assistant Secretary of Defense for Installations and Logistics proposed that the Navy aircraft storage and disposal centre at Litchfield Park, 150 miles north of Davis-Monthan, be closed and its function combined with that of the 2704th in a single manager operation. The Defense Supply Agency opened an office at Davis-Monthan to handle the sale of both Navy and Air Force surplus aircraft and to reflect its new multi-service role the 2704th was redesignated, on 1 February 1965, the Military Aircraft Storage and Disposition Centre (MASDC).

# 2
# MASDC and Vietnam

The mission of the Military Aircraft Storage and Disposition Centre (MASDC, pronounced MAS-DIC) was formally defined, to 'Function as the Single Manager Operating Agency of the Executive Director (HQ AFLC), for the Single Manager (Secretary of the Air Force), to provide a single point operation for the Department of Defense and other government agencies for the accomplishment of processing and maintaining aircraft in storage; preparation of aircraft for one-time flight, or transfer, inspection; reclamation of aircraft/aircraft engines and components for inventory replenishment and/or special projects; processing of aircraft/aircraft engines and residue for disposal; administration of sales and/or service contracts with foreign governments, other government agencies and commercial contractors; and performance of field level maintenance on selected aircraft systems and components as directed.'

An Interservice Agreement providing for services to be performed for the Navy by MASDC, was signed by General Mark E. Bradley, Jr, USAF, Commander AFLC; and by Rear Admiral Allen M. Shinn, US Navy, Chief, Bureau of Naval Weapons. Consequently, a Navy Field Service Office was established at MASDC and the move from the Naval Air Facility at Litchfield Park began.

The first Navy aircraft arrived at MASDC on 13 January 1965 and over the next twelve months over 800 more were delivered. The Navy decided to send 500 of these by truck, because it would have cost $4,000 to strip away each aircraft's preservative cover and prepare it for a 150-mile flight south-east to MASDC, only to be put into preservation again. With a comparative trucking cost of $350 per aircraft, the operation saved the government more than a million dollars.

The Navy's Industrial Air Department (AID) worked out the details of the actual loading. Each plane was carefully balanced so that it could be safely picked up by hook and crane for a safe ride on its journey by truck. Care had to be taken that each plane would have adequate clearance of concrete abutments of overpasses and underpasses along the route and still remain on its side of the highway.

By the end of 1965 817 Navy aircraft had arrived at MASDC, as follows:

| | | | |
|---|---|---|---|
| EA-1E | 11 | F-10 | 1 |
| A-3 | 32 | F-11 | 3 |
| A-4A | 83 | H-13 | 1 |
| C-45 | 127 | H-19 | 27 |
| C-47 | 3 | OH-43 | 37 |
| C-54 | 16 | O-1 | 3 |
| C-119 | 10 | P-2 | 53 |
| C-121 | 54 | S-2 | 50 |
| F-1 | 5 | T-1 | 1 |
| F-3 | 46 | T-33 | 47 |
| F-8 | 77 | T-34 | 29 |
| F-9 | 90 | U-16 | 1 |

An extra 1,000 acres of land was added to the base, giving MASDC 2,729 acres in which to accommodate the 2,000 Air Force aircraft already in storage, the influx of Navy aircraft and the early model B-52 Stratofortress bombers, the first of which arrived on 11 May 1965.

The movement was not all one-way though; 154 aircraft departed MASDC for foreign customers, including seven HU-16As for Italy, two T-28As for Ecuador, two C-54Ds for Denmark and C-47s for Colombia, Argentina and Kenya.

In addition, many varied uses were being found for other surplus aircraft and parts. The Department of Agriculture was given several C-45s and a C-47 to use in an experiment to halt inroads of the screw-worm fly in the south-western states, where range cattle were being affected. Male flies were sterilised by exposure to cobalt rays and then air-dropped in boxes that open on contact with the ground. The sterilised flies would help curtail propagation of the species.

In another instance the Indian government asked for help in constructing the Rojasthan Canal, which is located in a desert area. A thousand two-wheel excavation carts were needed that would not sink into the sand and could be towed by camels. MASDC provided excess wide-tread aircraft tyres, wheels and axles for building simple yet effective 'sand buggies'.

Other uses included two KC-97 carcasses for a project involving an orbiting space station; a C-54 to NASA for satellite ground station calibration; another to the Army in support of the Nike-X programme; a C-121 to NASA for downrange instrumentation checking; aircraft parts to the North American Aviation Company for an experimental 'hoverbuggy', and J-73 engines to support F-86s of an Air Force Military Assistance Program.

By now the United States was fighting a war in South-East Asia. Tactical aircraft based in Thailand and South Vietnam were flying missions against the Viet Cong in the south and targets in North Vietnam, ably assisted by the Navy aircraft carriers in the South China Sea. In June 1965 they were joined by B-52 bombers flying 'Arc Light' bombing missions from Anderson AFB on Guam. The fast, jet-engined tactical aircraft were hardly ideal for the new counter-insurgency war and a call was put out for slower, propeller-driven types. Soon almost 400 vintage B-26 bombers, T-28 Trojan trainers and A-1 Skyraider attack aircraft were being pulled out of mothballs, for transfer to an overhaul centre where they would be modified for their new ground-attack role in Vietnam.

The venerable C-47 'Gooney Bird' was used for many years as a transport plane. Thirty years after its first flight the Air Force removed 33 from storage, equipped them with three 7.62 mm mini-guns, capable of firing 6,000 rounds per minute each, and sent them to Vietnam. They were used by the Air Commando Squadrons to protect isolated outposts and were dubbed 'Puff, the Magic Dragon', by those who had witnessed their awesome nocturnal display of firepower.

By January 1966 the B-52 bombers on Guam were in need of replacement engines and a request went to MASDC for 24 J57-29 power packs. This was the first of many such requests and the required parts were removed from the B-52s in storage and shipped to Guam. Seven RB-66B Destroyers were also despatched to join those already in South-East Asia, and by June 1966 MASDC had shipped 51,000 spare parts and engines in support of the air war.

Opposite: Douglas RB-66B Destroyer 53-0446 had suffered extensive spare parts reclamation by the end of 1966 and was later sold for scrap. *(Robert M. Cornwell)*

The MASDC inventory as of 30 June 1966 consisted of 3,825 aircraft; 2,929 Air Force, 803 Navy and 93 from the Army, who had begun to use the centre during the year. The majority of the aircraft belonged to the Air Force and included 478 T-33s, 177 F-86s, 186 C-119s, 215 C-97s and 1,003 B-47 Stratojets bombers. When viewed from the air, the B-47 fleet was an impressive sight. For the moment the long lines of bombers sat baking in the sun. Their fate was inevitable though; between 1946 and 1966 almost 14,000 aircraft had arrived for storage at Davis-Monthan and only 2,800 had flown out again.

MASDC soon settled into its new role as the joint services aircraft storage centre. Within a year, 26 per cent of the centre's work was directed towards Navy aircraft and although the Army only accounted for four per cent, its first project, the reclamation of 44 H-21 helicopters, yielded a million dollars' worth of spare parts.

Colonel I. R. Perkin became the new MASDC commander on 28 June 1966 and immediately set to work changing the centre's image to one of a gold mine in the desert — a bonanza worth millions to the people of the United States. In order to publicise the work of the centre and its value to the taxpayer, a twenty-minute film and brochure were produced, appropriately titled *Desert Bonanza*.

Colonel Perkin also arranged the movement of a number of museum-type aircraft held at the centre, to an area near the perimeter fence, along Golf Links Road, where they could be seen by the general public. He was also a driving force behind the concept of an air musuem for Tucson, which was presented to Pima County in 1966 by a group of military and civilian aviation enthusiasts. The following year the Pima County Board of Supervisors appointed a committee to locate and obtain a site for the museum and in 1969 the Golf Links Road collection of 35 aircraft became the nucleus of the new museum. They were not moved to the new site until 1973, following inspection and certification by the Air Force Museum. In 1976 as an official Bicentennial event, the museum was dedicated and opened to the public. The collection, which by then had grown to 75, now contains almost 200 aircraft, some of which can be seen in no other museum. With the Air Force storage centre a matter of a few hundred yards away, the museum is guaranteed an inexhaustible supply of exhibits for the foreseeable future.

Meanwhile, back in 1966 the last remaining B-17 at MASDC, a DB-17P Drone Director aircraft, departed on a five-year loan to the International Flight and Space Museum in Ontario, California. It is rather ironic that twenty years earlier there were nearly 2,000 surplus aircraft awaiting the scrapper's torch at Ontario, including, of course, B-17s.

*E. O. Hatt Jr. NOV 15, 1987 WICHITA, KA*

Opposite: January 1967. The 1,000 strong Boeing B-47 Stratojet fleet has arrived and waits for the end. *(USAF Photograph)*

Right: These derelict Boeing B-52 Stratofortress bombers, photographed in 1975, were amongst 40 sold for scrap in 1983. *(USAF Photograph)*

Bottom: Air National Guard Republic F-84F and G Thunderstreaks stacked four high awaiting disposal in November 1958. *(Douglas D. Olson)*

Below: End of the line. A giant guillotine is used to cut this B-47 into smaller pieces for the smelter. *(USAF Photograph)*

With the war in South-East Asia in full-swing, some 92,507 direct labour hours, representing nearly fourteen per cent of MASDC's total, were spent supporting operations in 1967. 86 Navy A-4 Skyhawks and 74 F-8 Crusaders were despatched to various Naval Air Rework Facilities, for overhaul, modification and then transfer to Task Force 77 off the coast of Vietnam as combat loss replacements, or to Navy squadrons preparing for a tour of duty on 'Yankee Station'.

28 Navy Lockheed EC-121 airborne early warning aircraft were flown out to overhaul depots, where technicians worked around the clock to prepare them for use by the Air Force in South-East Asia.

High on the priority list were B-52 and B-66 engines. 266 were shipped to the B-52 squadrons and twenty to the B-66 units flying Electronic Counter Measures Support missions for the F-4s and F-105s heading north daily. The sixty early-model B-52s in storage had been virtually picked clean of spare parts by now and within a year they had all been broken up and scrapped.

The arrival ramp was also busy, with the first dozen F-86F Sabres being returned by Norway with two dozen more to follow. Eight huge C-124 Globemaster transport aircraft had also arrived as the fleet prepared for retirement. Most of them were suffering from wing defects and, in common with other reciprocating engined types such as the C-117, C-118 and T-29, the cost and scarcity of high octane fuel contributed to their replacement by jet-engined transport aircraft such as the C-141 Starlifter and C-5 Galaxy.

The first missiles began to arrive for storage in June 1967 with the retirement of the AGM-28A Hound Dog. They were delivered both by fly-in on B-52s during SAC training flights and by truck. SAC technicians accompanied the missiles to drain the dangerous anhydrous ammonia from the wing-mounted missile pylons and to remove certain parts of a restricted nature. Within a year 192 had arrived.

A total of 3,549 aircraft were in storage in June 1968, of which 622 had arrived over the preceding twelve months, including 53 Navy A-1E Skyraiders. These were soon transferred to the Air Force and shipped out to South-East Asia for use by some of the Special Operations Squadrons (formerly Air Commando Squadrons). The Skyraider was

Left: Douglas C-124C Globemaster 52-1069 was modified as a turbo-prop engine test bed. It cost $1,646,406 and spare parts worth $1,423,864 were removed before it was scrapped.
*(Robert M. Cornwell)*

Opposite: Strategic Air Command began to retire its Boeing B-47 Stratojet fleet in 1957. B-47E 53-6223 still wears its SAC badge after preservation in March 1967. *(Robert M. Cornwell)*

well liked and most suitable as a ground-support aircraft. It was rugged, could carry an impressive bomb load and could loiter over a target for much longer than the fuel-guzzling jets.

The B-47 fleet had begun its demise in December 1967 and soon 25 per month were undergoing reclamation. Out of the 1,000-plus fleet at least 463 had initially been earmarked for reclamation, with high priority parts such as 437 radar recording cameras and 874 magazines for the Environmental Science Services Administration, being removed first. Eventually the whole fleet would be sold for scrap to Allied Aircraft Sales of Tucson.

With more modern equipment being supplied to South Vietnam, some of their older types began returning to MASDC for storage. Eleven C-47Ds arrived late in 1968 followed by nine UH-34G and seven CH-34C helicopters in 1969. These were joined by seven C-119G transports being returned by Norway and two UH-16 Albatross amphibians retired by the Coast Guard who had also begun to use MASDC. One or two of the South Vietnamese C-47s and H-34s still survive at MASDC or in the local storage yards today.

The 1969 inventory was up slightly on 1968 to 3,576. Of these roughly 67 per cent were in regular storage, fifteen per cent were scheduled for reclamation, ten per cent were shells or hulks awaiting sale and seven per cent were of the Reclamation Insurance Type (RIT) status. This last category is conferred on aircraft set aside as a source for component or structural parts removal, to keep active aircraft flying. This provides a particularly useful source of spare parts for aircraft no longer in production and for which supply stocks have been exhausted. A prime example of this is the B-52, the last one of which came off the production line in 1962. Instead of having a service life of around ten years, it is likely to be in service until the turn of the century. Because of this unanticipated extension of its service life, some parts are no longer available and must be removed from aircraft already in storage. One such part is called an alligator clamp and can be removed from a B-52 at MASDC in a week, at a total cost of about $580. The supplier had quoted an eighteen-month lead time to remanufacture new clamps, at a cost of $100,000 apiece.

The B-47, however, was no longer in service and the 'save lists' of parts to be removed before disposal were consequently shorter. They could therefore be disposed of quicker and 300 had been scrapped by June 1969.

Opposite: The first Strategic Reconnaissance versions of the Stratojet were retired in October 1957. RB-47H 53-4280 was still present in October 1967. *(Author's Collection)*

When Richard Nixon took over the Presidency from Lyndon Johnson his policy regarding the South-East Asia War was one of 'Vietnamization' and gradual withdrawal. In anticipation of an early end to the war, MASDC received Operations Plan 'Pacer Harvest', which provided guidance for the expected input of aircraft after cessation of hostilities in Vietnam. Although the rundown of US air power in South-East Asia began almost immediately, it took until December 1972 and the appearance of B-52 bombers over Hanoi before North Vietnam agreed to sign the peace agreement. In the meantime Davis-Monthan Air Force Base was included in Operations Plan 'Garden Plot', which covered procedures in case of threat to USAF installations by anti-war protestors.

The two B-58 Hustler Bomb Wings began to send their aircraft to MASDC in November 1969 and by 16 January 1970 all 84 were in storage. One was given to the Pima Air Museum and two other record-breaking B-58s were given to other museums. *59-2458,* which had been flown in the 1962 round trip flight from Los Angeles to New York to Los Angeles, went to the Air Force Museum and *61-2059,* the one flown in the 1963 flight from Tokyo to London, went to the SAC Museum in Nebraska. The remaining Hustlers were sold to Southwestern Alloys in 1977 and broken up for scrap.

The first C-133 Cargomaster transport aircraft also arrived in 1970. When the Cargomaster entered service in 1957 it could carry twice the payload of the largest transport aircraft then in service. It was often used to transport Atlas, Thor and Jupiter missiles until, primarily due to metal fatigue, the fifty C-133s were retired by Military Airlift Command. Allied Aircraft Sales and Kolar Incorporated purchased the C-133s for scrap in 1973. They sold a handful of them as potentially flyable and with at least two preserved in musuems, around nine are still in existence.

Twenty CGM-13 Mace missiles arrived in June 1970 to join the Hound Dogs already in storage. The Mace was a surface-to-surface guided missile, fired from a hardened site or mobile launcher.

A temporary reduction in reclaimed aircraft sales was experienced following complaints by the Pima County Air Pollution Control department. Contractors were required to remove all carcasses of aircraft to private smelters at off-base locations, where they would be accountable to air pollution officials and would need smelters equipped with certain pollution controls.

*Opposite: Navy A-1E Skyraiders arrive at Cubi Point Naval Air Station from MASDC in March 1966. They will be overhauled before being flown out to aircraft carriers in the South China Sea. (U.S. Navy photograph)*

The MASDC inventory began to rise in 1971 and 1,970 aircraft were processed in, bringing the total in June 1971 to 4,605. At the same time MASDC began shipping out certain selected aircraft, destined for the countries in South-East Asia from which the United States was slowly withdrawing. Sixteen C-123 Providers left, to form part of 48 being supplied to the South Vietnamese Air Force. Ten UH-34G helicopters were shipped to Laos, presumably for use by the Central Intelligence Agency's airline Air America, which had used the type for years to support the anti-communist forces in the country.

Under Project 'Credible Chase', thirteen AU-23A gunship versions of the Pilatus Turbo-Porter were sent from MASDC to Thailand in 1972, for use in counter-insurgency missions. At the same time fourteen AU-24A Helio Courier gunships were sent to Cambodia, where they were used with great success against the Khmer Rouge prior to the fall of the Cambodian government.

Other gunships were going in the opposite direction and arriving for storage from South-East Asia. Three AP-2H Neptunes arrived from Heavy Attack Squadron (VAH) 21 at Cam Rahn Bay, from which they had flown over 200 missions, using their guns and bombs on road and river traffic in the 'Parrots Beak' area of the Mekong Delta. Two NC-123K Providers came in for demodification, following use in the 'Black Spot Program' testing new systems for future use by other types of gunship. Both were eventually supplied to the Thai Air Force as transport aircraft.

The year 1971 also saw the once-mighty B-47 fleet of 1,000 aircraft reduced to 56; 200 F-102A Delta Daggers undergoing reclamation and the arrival of 400 of the expected 540 TH-55A helicopters from the recently closed Army helicopter training installation at Fort Wolters, Texas. The year ended with an unexpected snowstorm of record proportions, which deposited five inches of snow over the centre on 8 December. Operations were brought to a standstill but, needless to say, the snowfall had melted by the next day.

The prototype Boeing 707-80 arrived for storage in June 1972, on behalf of the Smithsonian Institution. It was only one of 2,130 aircraft to arrive during the year, bringing the total inventory to 5,936 aircraft and 139 missiles. The all-time high of 6,080 was reached in June 1973 and comprised roughly 2,500 Air Force, 1,900 Navy, 1,500 Army and six Coast Guard. The largest number were 507 T-33s, followed by 484 TH-55As, 380 H-13s, 293 H-34s, 243 F-9s and 225 SP-2s. The Army, with nearly 1,400 helicopters, had arrived at last.

Opposite: Following its arrival in March 1967, Army
Sikorsky H-19D Chickasaw 56-1559 is shown in the early
stages of preservation, awaiting the application of 'Spraylat'
before joining the others on the right. *(Author's Collection)*

Below: Boeing B-47E Stratojet 53-6217 was photographed in
March 1969 with its tail guns still installed. It had previously
served with SAC's 9th Strategic Reconnaissance Wing.
*(Author's Collection)*

Opposite: Hulks of Navy A-1 Skyraiders awaiting sale for scrap in October 1968. *(U.S. Navy photograph)*

Below: Douglas B-26K Invader 64-17658 served with the 603rd Special Operations Squadron until its deactivation in July 1969. Preservation work has begun on the engines, although the majority of the B-26Ks were later scrapped. *(Lindsay Peacock)*

CREW CHIEF 1952

Opposite: Navy Grumman TAF-9J Cougar 131167 was used by training squadron VT-22 and retired in September 1969. A large number of the type were purchased for scrap by Southwestern Alloys of Tucson in July 1974. *(Lindsay Peacock)*

Bottom left: The New York Air National Guard retired North American F-86H Sabre 52-2094 in March 1965. It was transferred to the Navy in 1974 and converted to a remote-controlled QF-86H Drone at China Lake, California. *(Lindsay Peacock)*

Below: Beechcraft UC-45J Expeditor 51246 was used by the Navy at Pensacola in Florida, before retirement in 1969. *(Lindsay Peacock)*

Opposite: Lockheed T-33A 57-0606 on the arrival ramp on
17th November 1969. It is now preserved on the gate of
Williams Air Force Base in Arizona. *(Lindsay Peacock)*

Below: Grumman F-11A Tiger 141824 flew with the Navy
'Blue Angels' display team until it was stored at MASDC in
1969. It had returned to service again by 1973 and was
finally retired in 1975. It is currently on display at the Pima
Air Museum in Tucson. *(Lindsay Peacock)*

CREW CHIEF 1952

Opposite: Still fully preserved in November 1969, the final fate of this USAF Rescue Service Grumman HU-16B Albatross is unknown. *(Lindsay Peacock)*

Below: North American F-100A Super Sabre 53-1594 was photographed in 1969, following its retirement from the 118th Tactical Fighter Squadron, Connecticut ANG. It was later supplied to the Chinese Nationalist Air Force. *(Lindsay Peacock)*

Above: This Vought DF-8A Crusader was used as a drone director by composite squadron VC-8. It was stored in April 1969 and sold for scrap to Consolidated Aeronautics in July 1974. *(Lindsay Peacock)*

Opposite: Douglas YEA-3A Skywarrior 130361 was used by the Naval Air Test Centre and spent five years in storage before donation to the Pima Air Museum in Tucson. *(Lindsay Peacock)*

Opposite: Douglas F-10B Skynight 124610 was modified by the installation of an F-4B Phantom nose, prior to retirement in August 1968. It was later transferred to the Army for use as a spare parts machine and is one of five F-10s still in storage today. *(Author's Collection)*

Below: One of many Sikorsky CH-34C Choctaw helicopters used by the South Vietnamese Air Force, 54-3020 was returned to the States for storage in September 1969 and sold to Allied Aircraft of Tucson ten years later. *(Lindsay Peacock)*

Opposite: Douglas C-54Q Skymaster 56528 was retired by
Navy Antarctic Development Squadron VXE-6 in September
1966 and was sold to a civilian operator in March 1975.
*(Author's Collection)*

Bottom left: Still wearing full camouflage, Fairchild C-119C
Flying Boxcar 49-0156 was photographed in June 1970 and
later broken up for scrap. *(Author's Collection)*

Below left: One of the last few Northrop F-89J Scorpions
noted in storage in December 1969, 52-2127 formerly served
with the 134th Fighter Interceptor Squadron of the Vermont
ANG. *(Lindsay Peacock)*

Opposite: Almost 400 Convair F-102 Delta Daggers have been stored at AMARC since 1969. F-102A 56-1394 was operated by the 57th Fighter Interceptor Squadron at Keflavik, Iceland until retirement in May 1971. Its remains are still at AMARC today. *(Henry F. Carter)*

Below: Along with the rows of Convair F-102 Delta Daggers in the background, Lockheed EC-121K Constellation 137889 is being broken up and was sold for scrap in October 1974. *(Henry F. Carter)*

Above: These former Texas and West Virginia ANG Republic F-84F Thunderstreaks were transferred to the Navy and removed from MASDC in 1973, for use in explosives tests. *(Henry F. Carter)*

Opposite: 54-0691 was one of two Fairchild NC-123K Providers used in Vietnam as a part of Project Blackspot and was photographed shortly after arrival in May 1971. The aircraft was later supplied to the Royal Thai Air Force. *(Henry F. Carter)*

Overleaf: Douglas C-133 Cargomasters in storage in 1971. The nearest, C-133A 54-0137 from the 436th Military Airlift Wing, arrived on 7th January and was scrapped with the bulk of the fleet early in 1974. *(Henry F. Carter)*

Opposite: The 609th Special Operations Squadron used these Douglas B-26K Invaders on truck-hunting missions over the Ho Chi Minh Trail in Laos until their retirement in November 1969. The two nearest, 64-17660 and 665 were sold for scrap in 1976. *(Henry F. Carter)*

Below: These Piasecki (Vertol) CH-21B Workhorse helicopters were photographed soon after arrival in May 1971. They were purchased by Allied Aircraft Sales of Tucson in 1973 and are still present in their storage yard today. *(Henry F. Carter)*

Opposite: The Navy Missile Command put Douglas A-4C Skyhawk 145071 into storage in February 1971. It was supplied to the Singapore Air Force in February 1980. *(Author's Collection)*

Overleaf: These white-topped Boeing C-97G Stratofreighters of the New York Air National Guard were photographed in September 1972, following the removal of their engines and undercarriages. *(Henry F. Carter)*

Below: North American RA-5C Vigilante 151726 is one of 36 stored by the Navy between 1970 and 1979. 21 of the remaining 22 were sold for scrap in 1985. *(Author's Collection)*

Opposite: Another view of the storage area showing Army Hughes TH-55A Osage helicopters, Grumman OV-1 Mohawks and Cessna T-41A Mescaleros. Navy H-34 helicopters, F-8 Crusaders and SP-2 Neptunes are in the distance. *(Henry F. Carter)*

Bottom left: The Army had retired nearly 500 Hughes TH-55A Osage training helicopters by September 1972. Two rows of U-6 Beavers are in the foreground, with acres of B-52 bombers in the distance. *(Henry F. Carter)*

Below left: A view across the storage area towards the processing shed on 21 September 1972. Nearest are rows of Navy H-46 Sea Knight helicopters, with Air Force F-100s, F-84s and F-102s in the distance. *(Henry F. Carter)*

Overleaf: Douglas C-124C Globemaster 11 52-1022 of the 164th Military Airlift Group, Tennessee ANG was amongst 100 of the type retired in 1972. *(Henry F. Carter)*

Opposite: Not all the Cargomasters were scrapped in 1974. At least eight preserved or civilian-owned examples are still in existence today. *(Henry F. Carter)*

Below: The Marines placed 70 Boeing Vertol H-46 Sea Knight helicopters in storage in 1971 and 1972. Most were returned to service in 1974. *(Henry F. Carter)*

Opposite: Still bearing the markings of the South Vietnamese
Air Force in 1972, Sikorsky UH-34G Choctaw 140122 was
sold in March 1977 after eight years in storage. *(Henry F. Carter)*

Below: The Army had replaced its Hiller OH-23 Raven
helicopters with more modern types by the end of 1973. OH-
23D 61-3134 was one of many sold in March 1974.
*(Henry F. Carter)*

Opposite: Lockheed F-104D Starfighters 57-1332 and 1333 shortly after their arrival in December 1973. *(Author's Collection)*

Below: Navy Fleet Reconnaissance Squadron VQ-1 sent Lockheed C-121J Constellation 131654 into storage in 1974. Seven years later it departed to a civilian owner in California. *(Author's Collection)*

The obsolete Globemaster fleet was not required for preservation and by September 1972 the dismantling process had begun. C-124C 51-0123 of the Air Force Reserve 915th Military Airlift Group is nearest. *(Henry F. Carter)*

# 3
# The last decade

With America's involvement in the Vietnam War at an end and 6,080 aircraft in storage, the question was, what to do with them all?

One innovative idea was to replace the Air Force's subscale Firebee One and Two aerial targets with life-size surplus aircraft. The F-102 Delta Dagger possessed a marked silhouette likeness to the enemy Su-19, MiG-23 and MiG-25 and they were available off-the-shelf from MASDC. The Air Force awarded the Sperry Corporation a contract in 1973 to convert 215 F-102s into remotely-controlled target drones. The rebuild programme was called 'Pave Deuce' and the F-102s were de-preserved and ferried to the Sperry facility at Crestview, Florida, and, from 1978 onwards, to their local Litchfield Park factory. They were then stripped out and modified to fly by remote control, ending their days by being shot down over the White Sands Missile Range, in the New Mexico desert, or over the Gulf of Mexico.

The Army had decided that the vast increase in their helicopter inventory, as a result of the Vietnam War, meant that they could now do away with some of the older types in storage at MASDC. Consequently 1974 saw the first sale of some of the 500 H-13 Sioux and 400 H-23 Raven training and observation helicopters. A large number were sold to civilian owners and many more were supplied to various state agencies such as Forestry Departments, Civil Defense units, Police Departments and, for instruction purposes, to technical colleges and schools.

The Navy had 300 trainer versions of the F-9 Cougar carrier-based fighter in storage. The type had first flown in 1951 and was now obsolete. Southwestern Alloys purchased the first 100 offered for sale as scrap in 1974 and Sun Valley Aviation bought the rest two years later. The Navy also had over 100 T-1 Sea Star deck-landing trainers that were now obsolete. They went on sale in the summer of 1974 and were all purchased for scrap by Allied Aircraft sales.

To prevent combat-type aircraft falling into the wrong hands, they have to be de-militarised prior to removal from the centre. This process simply requires the purchaser to cut the wings and tail assembly off, thus rendering future reassembly and flight impossible. Generally speaking, transport aircraft and helicopters can be intact and therefore command a higher price. They have usually been subject to spare parts reclamation though and need careful restoration before certification by the FAA. One such type was the C-54 Skymaster, the military version of the four-engined DC-4 commercial transport aircraft. The first of eighty went on sale in 1974, with many being purchased for conversion to fire-fighting water bombers. One C-54, known as the 'Sacred Cow' and used by Presidents Roosevelt and Truman, was saved and sent to the National Air and Space Museum in Washington, D.C.

Aircraft still arrived for storage, although in fewer numbers than before. One interesting type to arrive was the WB-57F Canberra, eight of which had been retired following the 58th Weather Reconnaissance Squadron's disbandment on 1 July 1974. They had been greatly modified with new wings of 122 ft span, twice that of normal, and two huge TF-33 Turbofan engines. They were used for very high altitude reconnaissance and air sampling duties and a handful are still preserved in storage today.

The last two C-124 Globemasters also arrived during the year from the Georgia Air National Guard. One of the pair left in August 1975 for the USAF Museum and the rest of the fleet, minus their engines and undercarriages, was sold in 1976 for scrap. The second of the pair also escaped the axe and was sold to a civilian buyer, who flew it to Las Vegas, Nevada, and had it painted blue and white. It has remained there ever since.

Another transport type which began its retirement in 1974 was the Convair T-29, 86 of which arrived over the year. They continued to arrive until the end of 1975, when there were 300 of them in storage. The following year the sales of the type began and many found their way onto the civil market.

The Air National Guard also retired its last fifty F-100C Super Sabres during 1974. At the end of 1975 the first of 350 D and F models would begin to arrive, earmarked to follow in the footsteps of the last F-102s.

The year 1975 saw the final collapse of South Vietnam, but not before over 120 South Vietnamese Air Force aircraft had flown out to Thailand. These included 25 A-37B Dragonfly ground attack aircraft, which were sent to MASDC in June and July. Fourteen C-130 Hercules transports had also escaped to Thailand and Singapore and four of these also arrived at MASDC in 1976.

*Opposite: C-124C Globemaster 52-0956 was retired by the 116th Military Airlift Group of the Georgia ANG in December 1972 and sold for scrap in 1976. (Henry F. Carter)*

*Below: After service in Vietnam with Navy Heavy Attack Squadron VAH-21, Lockheed AP-2H Neptune 135620 returned to the States for storage in June 1969 and was given to the Pima Air Museum in June 1975. (Author's Collection)*

Almost seventy USAF C-118 Liftmasters were retired to MASDC in 1975. Most of them were sold the next year to civilian operators, although a few were transferred to the Navy. The Liftmaster was the first Military Airlift Command aircraft to fly the Atlantic nonstop. In 1964 they were added to MAC aeromedical evacuation units in the United States. They were used in Europe and the Pacific, including Vietnam, for evacuation of patients from combat areas and from theatre points of pickup. Their replacement is the jet-equipped C-9 Nightingale, the military version of the DC-9 airliner.

The last C-119 Flying Boxcars were retired by the Air Force and Marine Corps in 1975. The majority had been sold for scrap by 1979, although five still remain in the RIT area of MASDC today. Many C-119Gs were converted to AC-119G Shadow and AC-119K Stinger gunships and used in Vietnam. The G models were used to support troops in contact with the enemy and for airbase defence; the K

models were used almost strictly in the truck-hunting role over the Ho Chi Minh Trail.

The Navy's A-6B Intruder appeared at MASDC in July 1975, when two were processed in from Attack Squadron 34. They remained for three years until they were flown out for conversion to A-6Es and return to service. Since then another fifty A-6s have come and gone from both Navy and Marine units.

Surplus Air Force and Army utility aircraft were offered for sale in large numbers from 1975 onwards and nearly all took up civilian registration. These included fifty U-10 Couriers and 200 U-6A Beavers.

Supplies of aircraft to friendly governments continued during 1975 and a score of T-33s and six F-104s were withdrawn from storage and flown to Taiwan to join the Chinese Nationalist Air Force. This continued into 1976, when the 27 A-37B Dragonflies that had survived the fall of South Vietnam were supplied to South Korea. They were supplemented in 1977 by six C-123 Provider transport aircraft, retired earlier by the Alaskan Air National Guard. 1975 also saw the despatch of the last F-89 Scorpion from MASDC to the Air Force Museum and the arrival of the first Navy F-4J Phantom. The aircraft, a YF-4J converted from an F-4B, was recently given to the Pima Air Museum and restored by Mr Bob Bush, a Tucson resident.

Several large aircraft sales took place in 1976, consisting mainly of reclaimed fighters and bombers. The Navy no longer had any use for its TF-8A Crusader training aircraft and Consolidated Aeronautics, a local scrapyard, purchased fifty of them. The Sun Valley Aviation Company of Phoenix purchased some 150 Navy TF-9 Cougar fighters and 25 EB-66 Destroyers. The latter were light tactical bombers, modified by the Air Force and used extensively over North Vietnam by their Electronic Warfare squadrons. Sun Valley Aviation also purchased a handful of derelict F-102s and obtained 100 more in 1977.

The B-58 Hustler bombers which had been in storage since 1970 came under the hammer in 1977 and all 82 were purchased by Southwestern Alloys. They were towed across to their yard just outside the perimeter fence of MASDC, broken up and melted down into ingots in their furnace.

Sixty HH-43F Huskie helicopters were purchased by Allied Aircraft in 1977. It was the first helicopter used by the Air Force especially for airborne fire-fighting and crash-rescue operations. Allied had also bought two dozen OH-43D Marine Corps versions five years earlier. One of each are currently on display at the nearby Pima Air Museum.

Opposite: North American T-2B Buckeye 155220 was operated by the Headquarters Marine Corps Air Station Detachment prior to its retirement in May 1977. It remains derelict in AMARC today. (Author's Collection)

Below: Convair F-102A Delta Dagger 56-1122 was used by the 159th Fighter Interceptor Squadron, Florida ANG before being stored in 1974. It was converted to a PQM-102B remote controlled target drone in 1980. (Author's Collection)

The year 1977 also saw an upgrading of the centre's processes for examining reclaimed parts. It is necessary to be able to determine which spare parts are serviceable for re-use, from among those that are damaged or worn out. The two inspection processes then in use were a liquid penetrant test and a magnetic particle inspection. The liquid penetrant examination of aircraft parts was carried out by placing the part in a dye bath, which would reveal cracks inside the item when the part was exposed to a black light. This process was used for parts composed of aluminium, stainless steel and other materials which cannot be magnetised. Parts composed of metals which could be magnetised were subjected to the magnetic particle inspection. The part to be inspected would be coated with powdered steel shavings mixed with kerosene and when it was exposed to black light the cracks would show up as lines.

Three new processes were then introduced; X-ray inspection, ultrasonic inspection and 'eddy current' inspection. The X-ray machine used to inspect aircraft parts

was much more powerful, at 150,000 volts, than medical machines. In the ultrasonic inspection, fluid was put on the part, and high frequency sound waves sent through the item registered pulses on a scope, to indicate whether or not there was a flaw in it. Lastly, the eddy current technique was used by measuring the pattern of flow of an electric current thrust into the part.

By the end of 1977 1,424 aircraft were awaiting reclamation; the largest number being 171 Navy T-33s. 523 aircraft were awaiting sale, transfer or donation to appropriate agencies and 2,355 aircraft and helicopters were in storage. Times had changed, though, and the majority of the stored aircraft, 1,108, belonged to the Navy, with 678 Air Force, 563 Army and six Coast Guard. Amongst the Navy aircraft to arrive in 1977 were seven S-3A Vikings. The S-3 was taking over the anti-submarine search and strike role from the S-2 Tracker and 161 of the latter were in long-term storage, with another 116 undergoing reclamation at the end of the year.

It was indeed fortunate for the Royal Australian Navy that so many Trackers were preserved after retirement. On 4 December 1976, a hangar fire at the Naval Air Station at Nowra destroyed the Royal Australian Navy's S-2E Tracker squadron. After much deliberation and a detailed survey of the mothballed S-2Es at MASDC, the Australian government decided to buy sixteen replacement S-2Gs, which were equipped with a more modern anti-submarine sonics system. The first four were depreserved and on the washrack by 7 February 1977; on 16 March, a mere five weeks later, all sixteen were lined up at North Island Naval Air Station, San Diego, ready to return to Australia on the Aircraft Carrier HMAS *Melbourne*.

In 1978 Strategic Air Command retired sixty of its older B-52 D and F models to MASDC. At the same time the Texas Air National Guard retired the last KC-97Ls from service. Over 600 of the type had been retired to MASDC over the years. They have proved surprisingly popular in the aircraft sales, despite the government requirement that the

purchaser remove the refuelling boom and pumps from the fuel tanker versions.

Helicopter sales resumed in 1978 with the first of 300 obsolete TH-55A trainers being put out to tender. Foreign military sales also continued with 35 F-8H Crusaders going to the Philippine Air Force.

One of the more interesting types of aircraft to arrive in 1979 was the EB-57E Canberra, retired by the 17th Defense Systems Evaluation Squadron at Malmstrom AFB, Montana. They were equipped with the latest devices for jamming and penetrating air defences and used to simulate an enemy bomber force, attempting to find gaps in the air defence systems. The final examples of the EB-57 were retired by the 134th DSES, Vermont ANG, in 1982.

Boeing and McDonnell-Douglas both fielded two prototype aircraft for the Advanced Medium STOL Transport (AMST) competition in the early 1970s. Both types underwent testing and evaluation at Edwards AFB, by the manufacturers and Air Force Systems Command officials. The programme was suspended in 1979, following the withdrawal of Air Force funding and the two McDonnell-Douglas YC-15As arrived at MASDC in August 1979, followed by the two Boeing YC-14As in April 1980. One of each type has been loaned to the Pima Air Museum, on the condition that they be returned at 24 hours' notice if required.

The Air Force Reserve began to retire its C-123K Providers in June 1980 and at least one has since appeared on the civil market, in the colours of one of the fire-bomber companies. Two or three others have been withdrawn from storage, allegedly for use by certain government agencies for tasks involving flights to various South American countries.

The phase-out of the F-105 Thunderchief also began in the summer of 1980 when the 35th TFW at George AFB, in California, replaced its F-105G Wild Weasels with the F-4G. There were still a couple of years to go before the last would retire, having given stalwart service for over two decades, including the years of war in South-East Asia from which 397 of them did not return.

Visitors to MASDC in September 1981 had to blink and look again at the sight of seventeen American Airlines' Boeing 707s parked on the arrival ramp. They were the first of over 130 civilian Boeing 707s purchased by the Air Force, including the bulk of the Trans World Airlines fleet. All are being preserved in storage, after the removal of their engines and vertical and horizontal stabilisers, for future use by the

Amongst the preserved Lockheed C-130A Hercules is 57-0462, which arrived in May 1976 after service with the West Virginia ANG.
*(Author's Collection)*

KC-135 tanker fleet. The commercial carriers could no longer operate the Boeing 707s economically and the Air Force bought them for between $\$\frac{1}{2}$ and $1 million each. Spare parts worth many times that amount have been removed from each aircraft.

On 12 January 1982 the first F-106A Delta Dart arrived for storage, from the 48th Fighter Interceptor Squadron. Over 100 had arrived by December 1985 when it was announced that, under an Air Force programme called 'Pacer Six', about 200 F-106s would be converted to drones and used as aerial targets by the Air Force and Army. The Air Force began replacing the F-106s with the F-15 and the last few squadrons should complete the phase-out by 1988. Tactical Air Command plan to begin flying the first drones in 1988 and continue using them through 1995.

As a follow-on to the 'Pave Deuce' F-102 drone conversion programme, Sperry's Defense and Space Systems Division began converting the first of eighty F-100 Super Sabres to QF-100 drones in 1983. In addition, Flight Systems Incorporated at Mojave, California, have commenced the conversion of 209 more.

Sales of Navy aircraft have done rather well in recent years, with eighty S-2 Trackers and 48 E-1 Tracers — the latter an airborne early warning version of the S-2 — being sold to Consolidated Aeronautics in Tucson. Although all had suffered spare parts reclamation, they were offered for sale as potentially flyable. Despite the fact that one or two S-2s have been acquired by warbird enthusiasts, the only current commercial market for them is the fire-bomber operators. A large number of S-2s are already in service with the California Division of Forestry and their counterparts in Canada and France. A number of South American countries have also taken an interest in MASDC's stocks of surplus S-2s. In 1981 Grumman overhauled and supplied Trackers to Brazil and then in 1982 to Uruguay. More recently they have done the same with S-2s destined for the Peruvian Navy.

A-4 Skyhawk stocks at MASDC were reduced by around 100 in 1983. Allied Aircraft won a contract to crate and ship sixteen TA-4Bs to Singapore, who had received an initial batch of A-4Cs in 1980. 88 more were removed to an overhaul facility where forty complete examples were to be made for the Air Force of Malaysia.

The summer of 1983 also saw fifteen ex-Navy F-4J Phantoms fly out for overhaul, prior to despatch to England to add another Phantom squadron to the Royal Air Force. This reinforced the RAF Phantom strength, spread thin by the need to maintain a squadron at operational readiness on the Falkland Islands.

Portugal was next on the list to receive surplus Navy aircraft. Thirty A-7As were crated and sent to the Vought Corporation's factory in Dallas for modification into 24 A-7Ps and six TA-7Ps.

As fast as the Navy reduced their inventory at MASDC, more aircraft arrived to increase it again. From 1983 onwards more A-7s have been retired, together with over 100 Navy and Marine Phantoms. At least sixty H-1 helicopters and thirty T-28s have also arrived from various training establishments, together with the first early model P-3A Orion patrol aircraft. Some of the P-3s are earmarked for transfer to the Customs Service, while reclamation has already begun on others.

The Air Force has also been busy and forty B-52s have been sold for scrap, leaving around 230 others still in storage. As a part of the Strategic Arms Limitation Talks the B-52s have to be chopped up and left for 120 days so that Soviet satellites can verify their destruction.

In 1984 the Air Force also found a use for two of the DC-130 Hercules transports which had been used to launch remote-controlled drones in Vietnam and retired in 1979. The Aeronautical Systems Division 4950th Test Wing at Wright-Patterson AFB requested them for use as testbed aircraft for new electronic components. The idea saved the Air Force about $28 million, the basic price of two new C-130s.

The Air Force decided to attempt to change MASDC's 'aircraft boneyard' image in 1985 and renamed the centre The Aerospace Maintenance and Regeneration Centre (AMARC). This change also reflected an addition to the workload of the centre with the development of an aircraft contingency withdrawal programme. This is designed to supply the armed forces in a national emergency with mission-capable aircraft on short notice.

The centre still continues its traditional mission of storage and 1986 saw the arrival of the last C-123s and O-2s in the Air Force inventory, together with over 100 T-39 Sabreliners. The Coast Guard are making more use of the centre and have recently put some of their HC-130Bs into storage, so that the engines can be removed and fitted to new replacement HC-130s as a cost-saving measure. They have now been joined by at least a dozen Coast Guard H-52 helicopters.

The Marine Corps began to retire some of its early AV-8 Harrier vertical take-off aircraft in late 1985 and the total has now reached over thirty. The first Air Force Phantoms

Once used by the Pacific Missile Test Centre, Lockheed EC-121K Constellation 137890 departed for display at Tinker AFB, Oklahoma in October 1985, after six years in storage. *(Author's Collection)*

have arrived in the shape of thirteen F-4Es, although their stay promises to be brief and the Special Test C-130s from Hickam AFB are another recent arrival.

Throughout the 1970s and early '80s the number of aircraft in storage has steadily declined and the AMARC inventory is now around the 2,500 mark in an area increased to 3,000 acres.

The processing of aircraft into storage has changed since the early days of the B-29s, but is no less a complex procedure. On arrival all explosives, such as ejection seat charges, are removed, together with any pilferable or particularly valuable items. The aircraft is then washed to remove industrial or marine residues and inspected for corrosion.

Opposite: Only two of the 1,000 strong B-47 fleet remain at AMARC today. RB-47H 53-4304 and B-47E 51-5251 are in poor condition. *(Author's Collection)*

Below: One of the last Boeing KC-97L Stratotankers in service, 53-0304 was retired by the 181st Air Refueling Squadron, Texas ANG in April 1978 and sold to DMI Aviation in June 1984. *(Chris Allen)*

Navy aircraft, especially those on aircraft carriers, have been exposed to corrosive salt air and require anti-corrosion treatment. The aircraft is then towed to the Preservation Farm where mechanics drain the engines and hydraulic lines of oil. They also drain the fuel from the aircraft and then pump in a lightweight oil, which is again drained, leaving a protective oil film in the lines and tanks to protect them from drying out or corroding.

Engine intakes and exhausts are then covered with paper and any seams, inspection hatches, openings and rubber seals in the upper half of the aircraft are taped. The paper, tape and any fragile surfaces such as canopies and radomes are then sprayed with a heavy plastic-like material called 'Spraylat'; first with a coat of black and then with white to reflect sunlight. Wheel-wells, drainage holes and other openings under the aircraft remain open to allow circulation of air and minimise condensation.

Apart from protecting the aircraft from dust, sand and the elements, the main purpose of the 'Spraylat' is to maintain the internal temperature of the aircraft at only about five

degrees hotter than the surrounding air. Without such protection the inside of an aircraft could reach 200°F, causing damage to rubber parts and functional components. Unlike the B-29 cocoon, the 'Spraylat' can be easily peeled off should the aircraft be required to fly again.

Once the preservation process is completed the aircraft is moved into the desert. Ninety days later it is inspected again to ensure the preservative is still intact, then every 180 days until the aircraft has been stored for four years. At that time the aircraft is depreserved and all systems are inspected to make sure there has been no damage.

This method of preservation is currently undergoing change and AMARC has two full-time engineers in its desert laboratory undertaking research in aircraft preservation. Tedlar Tape is now being used, which does not require the usual 'Spraylat' coating, and a saving of seven man-hours and $620 per aircraft is the result. Funding is awaited for new aircraft covers for aircraft with a high probability of withdrawal and the savings in tape and 'Spraylat' could, in the case of the F-4, amount to $1,400 per year.

During Fiscal Year 1985 $301 million worth of spare parts was returned to military warehouses, an increase of 74 per cent over Fiscal Year '84. 173 aircraft were reclaimed for spare parts, an increase of 49 per cent over the previous year. This is the area in which AMARC justifies its existence.

For every dollar spent on its upkeep in 1984, AMARC was able to return to the government $13.18. Because of the increased re-utilisation of parts and aircraft, particularly in the form of target drones, that figure in 1985 jumped to $26.54 saved for every dollar spent. The bottom line for the US Treasury and the American taxpayer is that, in 1985, the value of all the returns to Department of Defense inventories from AMARC was over $0.5 billion.

The 621 civilians in AMARC's 623 member work force were complimented on 7 July by Colonel Edwin H. Moore, as he relinquished command of the centre to Colonel Herbert W. Grounds. 'I couldn't have asked for a finer group of people,' he said. 'They all sweat Air Force blue.'

Opposite: Immaculate civilian Globemaster N3153F preserved in Las Vegas, Nevada. This C-124C was formerly 53-0044 of the Georgia ANG and is one of the few of the type to escape the smelter. *(Author's Collection)*

Below: Grumman S-2 Trackers awaiting sale in November 1981. Almost 800 of the type have passed through the centre since the Navy joined MASDC in 1965. *(Chris Allen)*

Above: Beechcraft UC-45J Expeditor 51312 was the last C-45 to leave MASDC and departed for a museum in California in 1983. *(Author's Collection)*

Opposite: Ready to depart to an overhaul facility prior to transfer to the South Korean Navy, this Grumman S-2E Tracker 152822 was in storage from 1974 to 1981 and still wears the markings of Navy Anti-submarine Warfare Squadron VS-82. *(Author's Collection)*

Opposite: The last Marines Lockheed T-33 to be sent for storage. 138078 arrived in October 1975 and is still present today. *(Chris Allen)*

Below: A line of derelict Navy Vought F-8 Crusaders from Fighter Squadron VF-191 and Photographic Reconnaissance Squadron VFP-63, awaiting sale in 1981. *(Chris Allen)*

Above: The Marine Corps retired Douglas C-117 Skytrooper 50796 in October 1974. It was sold for scrap with others of the type in May 1982. *(Chris Allen)*

Opposite: Douglas TC-117D Skytrooper 17160 was purchased by Allied Aircraft of Tucson in August 1976 after seven years in storage and was photographed by the author in their storage yard in January 1982. *(Phil Chinnery)*

Opposite: One of the few Lockheed SP-2E Neptunes to be sold to a civilian operator, N88487 was photographed at Tucson airport in January 1982. It had been stored at MASDC from 1969 to 1976 and was formerly 131410. *(Author's Collection)*

Below: This Grumman HU-16B Albatross amphibian was operated by the 135th Air Commando Squadron, Maryland ANG before its sale to Allied Aircraft in 1973. It is still present in their storage yard, just outside the perimeter of AMARC. *(Phil Chinnery)*

Opposite: The shield displaying an Eagle holding a bomb in its beak and the motto 'E Sempre L'Ora', identifies this derelict B-52 as a former member of the 96th Bombardment Wing. *(Phil Chinnery)*

Below: Boeing B-52E Stratofortress 57-0138 of the 22nd Bombardment Wing arrived in June 1969. It suffered extensive spare parts reclamation over the years and was finally sold for scrap and broken up in 1983. *(Phil Chinnery)*

Opposite: One of 22 USAF Convair C-131A Samaritans transferred to the Coast Guard and converted to HC-131As, 5783 was photographed in October 1982. *(Author's Collection)*

Below: The markings on the nose of Sikorsky SH-34J Seahorse 145701 identifies it as item 153 in sale 41-2200. It was offered for sale with 165 other aircraft and helicopters in May 1982. *(Phil Chinnery)*

Opposite: Grumman US-2C Tracker 133349 was retired by Navy Composite Squadron VC-5 in June 1971 and sold to Consolidated Aeronautics in February 1982. *(Phil Chinnery)*

Below: When photographed in January 1982, this Navy Vought F-8H Crusader had been in storage and undergoing spare parts reclamation for eight years. *(Phil Chinnery)*

Opposite: Two of the MASDC workforce removing parts from McDonnell F-101B Voodoo 52-0278 of the Washington ANG. A task best completed early in the day, in view of the high temperatures experienced in the desert. *(Phil Chinnery)*

Bottom left: This very colourful Sikorsky SH-34J Seahorse was processed into storage in December 1969 and is still present with two others in the Reclamation Insurance Type (RIT) area. *(Phil Chinnery)*

Below left: Twenty years after their retirement, Marines Sikorsky CH-37C Mojave helicopters are still to be found in one of the storage yards bordering AMARC. *(Phil Chinnery)*

Opposite: Stored in the RIT area, Boeing Vertol UH-46A Sea Knight 152492 has been picked clean of spare parts since its arrival in December 1971. *(Phil Chinnery)*

Below: Minus their vertical stabilisers and engines, these civilian Boeing 707 airliners are used as a source of spare parts for USAF KC-135 Stratotankers. *(Mary Jo Keller)*

Opposite: Another resident of the RIT area, General Dynamics F-111A 63-9777 was used by NASA until it was stored as a source of spare parts in July 1971. *(Phil Chinnery)*

Below: The effect on an aircraft's centre of gravity following the removal of its engines, is clearly shown on this Convair T-29. *(Phil Chinnery)*

Opposite: Purchased by Allied Aircraft Sales from the Navy
Storage Facility at Litchfield Park, prior to its closure in
1965, these Piasecki (Vertol) UH-25B Retriever helicopters
are still present in their storage yard today. *(Phil Chinnery)*

Below: The final resting place for many Sikorsky CH-34C
Choctaw helicopters; a storage yard near the perimeter fence
of AMARC. *(Phil Chinnery)*

Above: Many Navy aircraft are stored in the desert to keep
them from the salt-laden air of coastal Navy bases. Lockheed
S-3A Viking 158864 on the departure ramp in July 1983 is
about to return to service. *(Phil Chinnery)*

Opposite: The last Air Force unit to operate the Martin B-57
Canberra, the 'Green Mountain Boys' of the 134th Defense
Systems Evaluation Squadron, Vermont ANG, retired B-57C
53-3856 in December 1981. *(Phil Chinnery)*

Overleaf: Painted high visibility red and used by Boeing and the Air Force Flight Dynamics Laboratory for Control Configured Vehicle tests, NB-52E 56-0632 arrived in June 1974 and is still present today. *(Phil Chinnery)*

Opposite: The first Grumman E-2B Hawkeye Airborne Early Warning aircraft stored at AMARC by the Navy, 150532 served on the aircraft carrier USS Nimitz prior to its arrival in June 1980. *(Phil Chinnery)*

Below: Navy Training Squadron HT-18 began to retire its Bell UH-1 helicopters early in 1982. Helicopters require extensive preservation and liberal amounts of 'Spraylat' to prepare them for long-term storage. *(Phil Chinnery)*

Opposite: Seen in its shipboard pose with folded wings, this Grumman US-2B Tracker 136643 served at Alameda Naval Air Station prior to retirement in December 1978. *(Phil Chinnery)*

Bottom left: A long line of Republic F-105 Thunderchiefs in storage in July 1983. Following retirement many were earmarked for display, battle damage repair training and use in ballistics tests. *(Phil Chinnery)*

Below left: The introduction of more modern types of fighter aircraft led to the retirement of Marine Fighter Attack Squadron VMFA-531's F-4N Phantoms, including 153006 which arrived in November 1981. *(Phil Chinnery)*

Opposite: Secured to a pallet in July 1983 for shipment to an overhaul facility and eventual return to service, Sikorsky CH-3E 64-14228 was retired by the 11th Tactical Drone Squadron in January 1979. *(Phil Chinnery)*

Below: Despite the removal of a number of major spare parts since its arrival in September 1974, this Navy North American T-2B Buckeye is still protected against the desert sun. *(Phil Chinnery)*

Opposite: Purchased from MASDC by Consolidated Aeronautics, these Trackers will probably be used to supply spare parts for S-2s still in service with foreign air arms, or civilian fire-fighting organisations. *(Phil Chinnery)*

Bottom left: Although preserved on arrival in July 1982, Bell UH-1E 153762 has RECLM stencilled on its tail boom, indicating its future use as a spare parts machine. *(Phil Chinnery)*

Below left: This Bell AH-1J Sea Cobra 3-4412, was destined for the Iranian Army, but is now stored in the AMARC Corrosion Control Area. *(Phil Chinnery)*

Opposite: The Coast Guard have begun to make more use of AMARC in recent years. Their early HC-130Bs are being retired and the engines removed for fitting to newer models. *(Phil Chinnery)*

Below: With the red CCV B-52 at its centre, this aerial view shows a large part of the fighter storage area and some of the 230 B-52s currently in storage. *(Phil Chinnery)*

FIREBALL EXPRESS

Opposite: One of the three Lockheed VC-140B Jetstar V.I.P. transports that arrived in 1983. *(Phil Chinnery)*

Below: The Southwestern Alloys storage yard in June 1984, full of Convair T-29s awaiting their fate. The yard is not far from AMARC, seen in the distance. *(Phil Chinnery)*

Opposite: With the possibility of future commercial interest, a number of former Coast Guard HU-16E Albatross amphibians remain more or less intact in the local storage yards. *(Phil Chinnery)*

Bottom left: With practically every useful part removed, this former Marines F-4N Phantom will eventually be sold for scrap. *(Robert C. Bush)*

Below left: This F-4N was flown by the 'Black Knights' of Marine Fighter Attack Squadron VMFA-314 before retirement in March 1982. *(Robert C. Bush)*

Opposite: Over 400 obsolete Neptunes have been stored at AMARC since the Navy closed their own storage facility in 1965. The majority have been sold for scrap, a fate that will probably befall the remainder. *(Phil Chinnery)*

Below: A general view across the storage area towards the processing shed. The arrival ramp is on the far side of the shed and the RIT area beyond that. *(Phil Chinnery)*

Opposite: After ten years in storage, North American OV-10A Bronco 155485 returned to service with the Marine corps in 1985. *(Phil Chinnery)*

Below: Recently withdrawn from use by the Navy, these Vought A-7E Corsair 11s will probably return to service with their own Navy or be supplied to an Allied air arm. *(Duncan Cubitt/Flypast Magazine)*

Overleaf: On loan to the Pima Air Museum from AMARC is Boeing YC-14A 72-1873. *(Phil Chinnery)*

Opposite: Stored at AMARC on behalf of the Air Force Museum, Lockheed EC-121H Constellation 53-0535 wears the badge of the Aerospace Defense Command on its vertical stabiliser. *(Phil Chinnery)*

Below: A decade has passed since F-8J Crusader 150680 was retired from Navy Fighter Squadron VF-194. *(Phil Chinnery)*

AEROSPACE DEFENSE COMMAND

0·30535

Opposite: Obsolete RF-101C Voodoos, F-105 Thunderchiefs and B-52 Stratofortress bombers awaiting sale for scrap in October 1986. *(Duncan Cubitt/Flypast Magazine)*

Below: The tours of AMARC, organised by the Public Affairs Office of the 836th Air Division, usually begin with a look at the impressive CCV B-52 Stratofortress. *(Duncan Cubitt/Flypast Magazine)*

Above: Boeing YC-14A 72-1874 and McDonnell Douglas
YC-15A 72-1876 were unsuccessful contenders for the
Advanced Medium STOL Transport competition, to find a
replacement for the C-130 Hercules.
*(Duncan Cubitt/Flypast Magazine)*

Opposite: Fairchild C-119 Flying Boxcar 53-8083 of the West
Virginia ANG is one of the five remaining C-119s out of the
500 to pass through the centre over the years.
*(Duncan Cubitt/Flypast Magazine)*

Above: These two DC-130A Hercules were used to launch
radio-controlled reconnaissance drones by Navy Composite
Squadron VC-3 until retirement in 1979.
*(Duncan Cubitt/Flypast Magazine)*

Opposite: Despite having suffered extensive spare parts
reclamation, these Navy Douglas C-118B Liftmasters will
possibly be sold to civilian companies for restoration and
FAA certification. *(Duncan Cubitt/Flypast Magazine)*

Opposite: One of the latest types of aircraft to arrive for storage is the Marine Corps McDonnell Douglas AV-8 Harrier. At least a dozen AV-8A and 19 AV-8C had been withdrawn from use by the end of 1986.
*(Duncan Cubitt/Flypast Magazine)*

Bottom left: Former South Vietnamese Air Force C-47D 43-48415 has been in storage since September 1968.
*(Duncan Cubitt/Flypast Magazine)*

Below left: Former Coast Guard Fairchild C-123B Provider 4529 was retired in May 1972 and offered for sale by sealed bid as item 11 of sale 41-6304 on 7 May 1986.
*(Duncan Cubitt/Flypast Magazine)*

Opposite: The first Convair F-106A Delta Dart was retired in January 1982 and around a hundred are now in storage. 59-0083 is at the head of the row wearing the AMARC inventory number FN035. *(Duncan Cubitt/Flypast Magazine)*

Below: McDonnell F-4S Phantom 153881 served with Navy Fighter Squadron VF-161 on the USS Midway and was photographed on the arrival ramp in October 1986.
*(Duncan Cubitt/Flypast Magazine)*

# Tour Information

At the present time, tours of the centre are being conducted on a reservation basis only. On Monday and Wednesday mornings the tour is relatively short and includes a drive down the Davis-Monthan flight line and around the storage areas. Visitors on this tour are not allowed to leave the bus. For enthusiasts and photographers a four-hour photographic tour takes place at 08:00 on the second Saturday of each month and people are allowed off the tour bus to photograph aircraft. For further information contact the Public Affairs Office, 836th Air Division, Davis-Monthan AFB, Arizona 85707, USA. Telephone (602) 748-3358.

# Aircraft Type

*Quantity*

| Aircraft | Quantity |
|---|---|
| A-3 Skywarrior (Douglas) | 42 |
| A-4 Skyhawk (Douglas) | 35 |
| A-5 Vigilante (NAA) | 1 |
| A-6 Intruder (Grumman) | 20 |
| A-7 Corsair 11 (LTV) | 88 |
| PA-48E Enforcer (Piper) | 2 |
| B-47 Stratojet (Boeing) | 2 |
| B-52 Stratofortress (Boeing) | 228 |
| B-57 Canberra (Martin) | 35 |
| C-1 Trader (Grumman) | 24 |
| C-7 Caribou (DHC) | 9 |
| YC-14 (Boeing) | 2 |
| YC-15 (McDD) | 2 |
| C-47 Skytrain (Douglas) | 4 |
| C-118 Liftmaster (Douglas) | 29 |
| C-119 Flying Boxcar (Fairchild) | 5 |
| C-121 Constellation (Lockheed) | 3 |
| C-123 Provider (Fairchild) | 38 |
| C-130 Hercules (Lockheed) | 35 |
| C-131 Samaritan (Convair) | 46 |
| C-135 Stratotanker (Boeing) | 2 |
| C-137 (Boeing 707) | 148 |
| VC-140 Jetstar (Lockheed) | 2 |
| E-2 Hawkeye (Grumman) | 20 |
| F-4 Phantom (McDD) | 170 |
| F-8 Crusader (LTV) | 46 |
| F-9 Cougar (Grumman) | 1 |
| EF-10 Skynight (Douglas) | 5 |
| F-11 Tiger (Grumman) | 2 |
| F-14 Tomcat (Grumman) | 1 |
| F-84 Thunderflash (Republic) | 3 |
| F-100 Super Sabre (NAA) | 193 |
| F-101 Voodoo (McD) | 16 |
| F-102 Delta Dagger (Convair) | 10 |
| F-104 Starfighter (Lockheed) | 2 |
| F-105 Thunderchief (Republic) | 23 |
| F-106 Delta Dart (Convair) | 97 |
| F-111 (General Dynamics) | 7 |
| AH-1 Cobra (Bell) | 1 |
| UH-1 Iroquis (Bell) | 87 |
| H-3 Sea King (Sikorsky) | 1 |
| H-34 Choctaw/Seabat (Sikorsky) | 6 |
| H-46 Sea Knight (Vertol) | 2 |
| H-47 Chinook (Vertol) | 22 |
| HH-52 Seaguard (Sikorsky) | 14 |
| TH-55 Osage (Hughes) | 78 |
| TH-57 Sea Ranger (Bell) | 29 |
| H-60 Black Hawk (Sikorsky) | 2 |
| O-2 Skymaster (Cessna) | 163 |
| SP-2 Neptune (Lockheed) | 87 |
| P-3 Orion (Lockheed) | 28 |
| S-2 Tracker (Grumman) | 51 |
| T-1 Seastar (Lockheed) | 1 |
| T-2 Buckeye (Rockwell) | 2 |
| T-28 Trojan (NAA) | 75 |
| T-29 (Convair) | 7 |
| T-33 (Lockheed) | 125 |
| T-34 Mentor (Beech) | 20 |
| T-38 Talon (Northrop) | 13 |
| T-39 Sabreliner (NAA) | 118 |
| U-8 Seminole (Beech) | 24 |
| HU-16 Albatross (Grumman) | 6 |
| OV-1 Mohawk (Grumman) | 46 |
| AV-8 Harrier (HSA) | 31 |
| OV-10 Bronco (Rockwell) | 1 |

Total of 2,512, comprising 1,487 Air Force, 825 Navy, 186 Army and fourteen Coast Guard. Of the 2,512, 1,756 are in storage, 586 undergoing reclamation and 170 are sold or awaiting sale.